Success with
Citrus Fruit

D0271121

Sigrid Hansen-Catania

Editor
Karen Douthwaite

MEREHURST

Introduction

A breath of the South

Lemon and orange trees – who would not instantly associate these plants with a dream of the sunny south? Even as a balcony and patio gardener, using citrus plants in large containers will enable you to create Mediterranean surroundings. If you look after them carefully, following the appropriate care instructions given for the species, these plants from the warm southern countries will thrive here and even bear fruit.

In this guide, citrus plant expert Sigrid Hansen-Catania explains what it takes to grow citrus plants. She introduces the most suitable and attractive species and supplies easily understandable, tried and tested directions for planting, care, overwintering and plant protection. There are also lots of ideas for designing with citrus plants, plus useful information on the use of fruits and leaves as well as tips on buying individual species and varieties. You'll find some fascinating background information on citrus plants – their history as ornamental plants, their use in the kitchen and in healing – but most of all this book gives the perfect introduction to the fascinating world of citrus plants.

Wishing you much enjoyment and success in growing your own citrus plants.

Contents

Dwarf oranges combined with various foliage plants.

Lemon blossom.

Grapefruit.

The author

Sigrid Hansen-Catania studied gardening and has also studied the cultivation of ornamental plants in Mediterranean countries. She has been a gardening advisor for many years and is a specialist in several citrus plant companies on the island of Corsica. She works for various gardening periodicals and has published numerous articles on Mediterranean plants.

The photographers

Friedrich Strauss has a diploma in garden design. His gardening training was followed up with the study of art history. For many years now he has been taking photographs for well-known specialist gardening periodicals. Further photos are by other well-known garden and plant photographers (Credits, see p. 63)

The illustrator

Gyorgy Jankovics is a graphic design artist. He studied at art academies in Budapest and Hamburg and has produced illustrations of plants and animals for many other gardening and wildlife titles.

Important: Please pay particular attention to the *Warning and notes* on p. 61 so that your enjoyment of citrus plants will not be impaired.

Beautiful plants – fine fruits

The very long tradition of growing ornamental citrus plants started in splendid orangeries and noble gardens and has for some years been enjoying a revival on balconies and patios. Meanwhile, some of the edible varieties from the great family of citrus plants have attained worldwide importance.

Left: A stunning selection of Mediterranean plants on a patio: kumquat, calamondin orange and eucalyptus grouped in a variety of plant-friendly terracotta pots.

Above: Orange flower water, the famous old Arab flavouring medium is made from orange blossom.

Things to know about citrus plants

Mysterious origins

The history of citrus plants is not only mysterious but also quite extraordinary. To this day, hardly anything is known about the origins and sources of these plants, that have become indispensible as suppliers of delicious fruits. Citrus plants belong among the very oldest domestic plants that were originally only grown for decoration or for healing purposes. In China citrus plants were being cultivated as early as 2200 BC. A book called the "Yu-Kung" written at the time, referred to oranges and grapefruits. Oranges are even supposed to have been grown in the Hanging Gardens of Babylon. One of the oldest cultivated species was the citron (*Citrus medica*) that was already being grown in 700 BC in the Kingdom of Media (present day Iran). The Greek philosopher Theophrastus, a pupil of Aristoteles, wrote about the "Median apple" in the third century BC, that had become known due to Alexander the Great's Asian campaigns. To this day, according to an old Jewish custom, the 'Ethrog', a variety of the citron, is still presented as a symbol of *Hadar,* the biblical Tree of Splendour at the annual *Succoth* (Feast of Tabernacles). The Romans extended the cultivation of citrus plants across to Italy and the Roman poet

Virgil praised the Seville or bitter orange as the "most wonderful medium to combat poison that has been swallowed". The lemon tree often crops up as a motif in 1st century mosaics. It is, however, to the Arabs that these important plants owe much of their popularity – they introduced the first citrus plants to the Mediterranean region. In 1030 AD, the Arab sage and physician Avicenna (Ibn Sina) described in detail the Seville or bitter orange (*Citrus aurantium*) and its many uses as a healing agent.

The path to Europe

It is thought to be Portuguese merchants who, around 1500, brought the first sweet oranges from India and China to Europe – all citrus fruits known up until then had been sour or bitter. This was the time when an intensive distribution of citrus plants began in the Mediterranean world. Christopher Columbus took seeds of various different citrus plants with him to Haiti on his second journey to the New World. At the beginning of the 16th century, seeds were imported to Mexico, Brazil, Florida and, a little later on, to California. From Brazil they reached Australia, and English and Dutch people brought citrus seeds to South Africa in 1654. Today, citrus plants are present on all five continents.

Orangeries

Citrus plants were highly valued as ornamental plants very early on. The kings and noblemen of the Baroque period had orangeries built in their palatial gardens. In these buildings that were always equipped with large windows, orange, Seville or bitter orange and lemon trees were cultivated in large containers. This meant that the sensitive citrus plants could be grown in areas where growing them outside would have been imposssible due to unfavourable climatic conditions. While orange and lemon trees were mainly enjoyed for their beauty and grace, the edible bitter oranges - Seville oranges or "golden apples" as they were often known, - remained a rare delicacy for only the rich and mighty.

Citrus plants were the most popular ornamental plants up to the end of the 18th century because of their great value as decorative elements. In the 19th century, wealthy citizens also began to build their own winter gardens and greenhouses in order to grow citrus and other Mediterranean plants and harvest their fruits. This passion has been rediscovered over the last few years and citrus plants have become highly desirable large container plants for patios and balconies.

Citrus plants have been prized for their ornamental value for centuries.

Things to know about citrus plants

The tradition of ornamental citrus plants

The variety and beauty of citrus plants can be admired in numerous places of historical importance. Tuscany is one area that is rich in such historic sites. Although, even here, frosty temperatures are experienced in winter citrus plants are still grown in many places. The tradition goes back to the 15th century, the era of the famous Medicis who appreciated the therapeutic qualities of the citrus plants but also greatly prized their beauty. They surrounded their villas with gardens in which flowering and fruit-bearing citrus trees were the main features.

The garden of the Villa Castello in Florence

This garden is a living testament to the Renaissance art of gardening. Visiting the garden is like stepping back in time. With its 500 specimens, it must represent one of the largest collections of cultivated citrus plants in pots. Amongst them are some particularly rare varieties, such as a bitter orange with bizarre yellow-orange patterned fruit that was cultivated for the first time in Florence in 1640. Villa Castello is also home to one of the oldest terracotta vases dating from 1790 and with the original plant still growing in it. Villa Castello's citrus plants are overwintered in the *limonia*. This name is derived from the fact that Italians have a special preference for lemons, *limoni* in Italian, while the French prefer oranges and, therefore, use the term orangery. During the Second World War the limonia at Villa Castello was used as a hospital and many of the plants that were left to overwinter outside died during this period. Some of the trees were saved through renewed grafting. The success of this procedure owed a lot to the vigour of the old citrus plants. Today's visitors to the Villa Castello can still see the effects of those traumatic years in the citrus plants' carefully bandaged scars. Also in Florence, in the Boboli gardens of the Palazzo Pitti, about 200 citrus plants in old terracotta vases are grouped together to form a wonderful vista framed with fountains, statues and ponds. Added to the citrus plants of the Villa Castello, Florence boasts a total of about 1,000 specimens representing about 200 varieties in these two beautiful gardens.

The orangery of Versailles

The most important places to admire ornamental citrus plants in France are, of course, in the capital, Paris. Thanks to Maria de Medici, wife of Henri IV of France, more than 250 orange, lemon and lime trees were brought to France in 1615 and formed the basic stock of the Jardin de Luxembourg. The master gardeners commissioned with the task of looking after these trees, received detailed instructions for cultivation from their colleagues in Tuscany, techniques that are still practised to this day. The orangery at Versailles is one of the most famous places to appreciate the long tradition of citrus plants and is probably the most beautiful orangery in Europe. A walk around the splendid building is highly recommended if you are lucky enough to find it open during the summer. Back in 1654, when the building was completed, admirers were of the opinion that "If the King (Louis XIV) can dedicate such a beautiful building to his favourite plants, citrus plants, he must indeed be a great king." To this day, great receptions and celebrations take place in the orangery in summer. From 15 October to 15 May, however, this building becomes the place to admire the winter quarters of the Sun King's favourite plants,

The beautiful garden of the Villa Castello is home to one of the largest collections of ornamental citrus plants in the world.

among them as many as 650 orange trees alone. The temperature is kept as constant as possible, never less than 5°C (40°F) or more than 8°C (46°F). Once a month, over 1,000 plants are watered by hand and the building is ventilated daily to reduce humidity. In May, the 1,000 large plant containers are all carried back outside again into the gardens.

Orangeries of the world

Beautiful orangeries are not confined to France and Italy, they can be found in many countries of the world. Germany has some fine examples, including the Palace of Sanssouci in Potsdam (Berlin) and, in Leonberg, the Pomeranzengarten, one of the few Renaissance gardens in Europe to be restored according

to original plans. In Britain, Hampton Court Palace boasts two orangeries with King William's orangery still housing citrus trees in winter. The magnificent orangery at Tatton Park, Knutsford, Cheshire, has recently been restored and contains orange trees again, while that at Ham House, Surrey is thought to be Britain's oldest surviving orangery (17th century).

Things to know about citrus plants

Economic importance

Citrus fruits are now positioned in third place as the world's most popular fruits after bananas and grapes. Oranges in particular also occupy an important position in the food production industry. By far the largest share of the worldwide production of citrus fruits is processed into fruit juices. Many drinks and foods, such as fruit preserves and jam, contain extracts from citrus flesh and peel. The most important citrus fruits are oranges and mandarins, lemons and grapefruits. The agricultural area for cultivation of citrus fruits amounts to approximately 3.5 million hectares (8¾ million acres) worldwide. About seven per cent of citrus plantations are replaced with new plants every year as the old trees will often no longer produce an adequate yield. Citrus tree nurseries cultivate about 70 million young plants a year, for plantations worldwide. The cultivation of ornamental citrus trees is minimal by comparison.

Cultivation areas

Important areas for cultivation are the Mediterranean countries, for example, Italy (especially southern Italy and Sicily) but also France (southern France and Corsica) as well as a few areas of Spain and Portugal.

Oranges come from Spain (mainly navel and Valencia oranges) and Morocco. While oranges are available all year round, with the main season being from October to June, the best time for Sicilian blood oranges (Sanguinello or the almost pipless Tarocco) is February and March. Israel is also an important exporter of citrus fruits and is where the much prized Jaffa oranges, for example, come from. In Brazil, the production of oranges is counted economically among the country's major sources of income. The main part of the harvest is processed into orange juice for export. The main cultivation areas for grapefruits are Israel, Spain and Florida. Clementines are the only seasonal fruits as they can only be harvested from the middle of September to May. They come from Morocco, Spain, Israel, Turkey, Florida and France. Large quantities of cultivated clementines can also be found in Corsica. Lemons are exported mainly from Spain, Italy, Egypt, Turkey, Cyprus and the USA. It is surprising that Italy, the country that is so famous for lemons, and in particular the island of Sicily, exports only 150 tons annually, while Spain now delivers 100,000 tons per year.

The Verdelli process

In Sicily, lemons are harvested right into the summer, using a special cultivation method, known as the Verdelli process. The regular harvest period runs from the middle of September to May. To begin with, green fruit, later on, yellow (ripe) fruit is harvested. During the summer, in order to produce green lemons (verdelli) again, particularly large trees are deprived of any water whatsoever for 40 days from June onwards. This drought causes such stress to the plants that they are forced to produce a second lot of blossom in August/September of that year. To do this, the soil is removed from around the roots and all irrigation ceases. As soon as the leaves of the lemon trees begin to dry up, the roots are covered again with soil and they are watered. With this method, a more concentrated second harvest can be obtained in September and October of the following summer. As the weather is still warm, the lemons will often remain green but they are just as tasty and juicy as the fruit of varieties that are ready later on.

Delicious – and healthy too

Citrus fruits not only taste delicious but, due to their high

The Mediterranean countries are important cultivation areas for citrus fruits.

vitamin C content, they are of great importance in maintaining good health. Columbus already knew about this and is said to have taken along fresh lemons to combat scurvy on his second journey to the New World. The average vitamin C content of lemons is around 44 mg/100 g fruit juice, in oranges 59 mg/100 mg. Vitamin C raises the immune response of the body. One glass of lemon juice drunk in the morning before breakfast, according to Chinese doctors, is the best method to purify the liver and begin the day full of vigour. Lemon juice has been used for centuries as a treatment for fevers and hot lemon juice remains a tried and tested home remedy for colds and flu due to its anti-bacterial and temperature-lowering effect.

Vitamin C stimulates the formation of collagen (slowing down the skin's ageing process) and helps heal wounds. It also supports the elasticity of tissue walls. As well as vitamin C, citrus fruits contain vitamins A, B, E and P, and various trace elements. Vitamin C helps eliminate nicotine from the body. Smokers should, therefore, take in more vitamin C.

Botany

The structure of a citrus fruit:

(a) flavedo or epicarp (outer coloured portion),
(b) albedo or mesocarp (inner part of rind),
(c) Endocarp or pulp (fruit segments),
(d) pips

Because of the tendency for the creation of hybrids within species of one genus, but also between species of different genera, citrus plants are very difficult to place in a botanical system, particularly as there is a constant supply of new hybrids to take into account.

A difficult family

Citrus plants belong within the family of *Rutaceae*, a plant family that includes more than 1,600 species, arising mainly in the tropics and sub-tropics and divided into two sub-families, the *Rutaidea* and lemon-like *Citroidea*. The content of etheric oils is typical of all citrus plants. Among the *Citroidea*, that all originate from East Asia but have been cultivated for a long time in the Mediterranean area, are counted the three genera: *Citrus* with 16 species, for example the lemon (*C. limon*), the Seville or bitter orange (*C. aurantium*), the pampelmousse or pomelo (*C. maxima*), the citron (*C. medica*), the mandarin (*C. reticulata*), the sweet orange (*C. sinensis*), the grapefruit (*C. x paradisi*) and the lime (*C. aurantiifolia*). The genus *Fortunella* with only one species, the kumquat; and *Poncirus* with only one species, the Japanese bitter orange (*P. trifoliata*) that are mainly used as rootstocks for *Citrus* species. Using *Poncirus trifoliata* as a rootstock for Citrus results in plants that are less sensitive to cold.

Bush or tree

Citrus plants are – with the exception of *Poncirus trifoliata* – always evergreen, bush-like to tree-like woody plants that may grow to a height of 5-15 m (17-50 ft) in the wild. Even citrus plants in large containers may reach astonishing heights with increasing age, in spite of the reduced root development. The orange trees in the Jardin de Luxembourg in Paris are between 80 and 200 years old and are about 4 m (13 ft) high. In specialist citrus nurseries, you may find 50 year old orange trees that have reached heights of up to about 2.5 m (8 ft).

Shiny evergreen leaves

The leaves of citrus plants are simple, tough and shiny. They vary from light to dark green and are more or less elongated oval-shaped, slightly dentate at the edges and, depending on the age and species or variety of the plant, 7-18 cm (3-7 in) long. The small "wing leaf" at the base of the leaf is characteristic for many species. Very often, the species with a wing leaf in particular will also bear a very tough thorn (the bitter orange, for example). In the case of other species, such as the orange, the thorn is only vestigial, in clementines, mandarins and calamondin oranges the thorn is completely absent. Some varieties have a very characteristic shape of leaf which simplifies indentification. This is the case with the Japanese bitter orange, that is easy to identify due to its three-partitioned leaf. Nearly all citrus species have evergreen leaves, a sign of how well suited these plants are to the mild winters of their countries of origin. Only the Japanese bitter orange loses its leaves in the winter as a protective measure against the cold. If, however, temperatures sink below 10°C (50°F), many citrus species react by losing their leaves. This is normal and a sign of the winter rest phase. The lemon 'Meyer' (*Citrus limon x sinensis 'meyer'*) is considered to be particularly sensitive and will lose all its leaves at temperatures below 6°C (43°F). In the spring it will recover and put out shoots again.

Small but scented

The flowers of citrus plants are symmetrical and are composed of 3-5 sepals and 4-8 petals together, 20-30 anthers are arranged in a circle around the style. Their yellow pollen is distributed in the spring when the flower has opened completely. The flower is pure white, with tinges of violet in some species, for example in lemon blossom. The small, inconspicuous flowers release an intense scent that ranges from flowery-fresh (lemon) to heavy-sweet (orange).

Juicy and rich in vitamin C

Citrus fruits are easily distinguishable by their shape and size (citrons can weigh up to 2 kg [4½ lbs], while the fruit of the calamondin orange has a diameter of 3-4 cm (2 in). All have in common a high concentration of vitamin C. The fruit is typical for the species and allows exact indentification. The fruits are green to begin with and do not change colour to yellow or yellow-orange until they are ripe. The yellow-orange colour only occurs when the night-time temperatures are relatively cool. For example, clementines require night-time temperatures of around 12°C (54°F) in order to turn orange in their ripening phase (October to beginning of December). The green lime from the Caribbean, on the other hand, remains green because the temperatures there do not fall sufficiently during the night. The fruit itself is composed of the peel, the fruit flesh and the pips. The peel consists of two layers, the hard outer skin (flavedo) and the often spongy inner layer, the pith (albedo). The fruit flesh consists of a varying number of individual juicy segments that enclose the pips. In oranges there are 9-11, in grapefruits 12-15 and the number of pips will vary from one variety to another.

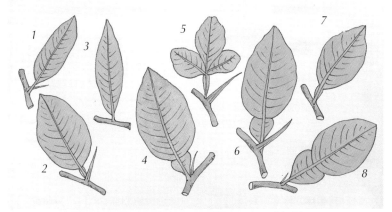

1 Kumquat (Fortunella japonica), 2 orange (Citrus sinensis), 3 kumquat (Fortunella margarita), 4 grapefruit (Citrus x paradisi), 5 Japanese bitter orange (Poncirus trifoliata), 6 bitter orange (Citrus aurantium), 7 mandarin (Citrus reticulata), 8 pampelmousse (Citrus maxima)

Things to know about citrus plants

Citrus fruits and their culinary uses

In days gone by, citrus fruits were rarely eaten in their raw state but used instead for their distinctive flavour in the preparation of many dishes. Documents originating from the 14th century show that citrus fruits were often used in the preparation of meat and fish dishes. One possible explanation for this is that the sweet orange, the clementine and the mandarin were not known then and all the other citrus fruits were too sour to consume raw. Citrus fruits are also processed and consumed as juice and in liqueurs (for example, in the world-famous Grand Marnier) and in other dishes (jams and marmalade). Not only the flesh of the fruit but also the etheric oils contained in the leaves, the candied peel (from both oranges and citrons), as well as orange flower water are all used for culinary purposes.

The orange

This flavourful and, thanks to its high content of vitamin C, very healthy fruit is extremely refreshing on account of its acid content. This large proportion of acid plays an important part, as the ratio between sugar and acid percentages is responsible for the flavour. If this ratio is not properly balanced, the fruit will taste insipid. A consistently warm climate, such as that in tropical regions, hinders the formation of acid, so fruit from these regions does not have such a good flavour. The introduction of the orange to Europe in the 16th century was of great importance for its cultivation. In the Mediterranean area, in particular, the differences in temperatures at the time of ripening, that is in the winter, create a sugar and acid ratio that makes the flavour outstandingly good. Once the ripening level is crossed, the sugar-acid ratio drops again. This explains why oranges taste best in the main season (see p. 39).

Clementines and mandarins

The main harvest time for clementines is from the middle of October to February (or the middle of autumn until late winter in other parts of the world). The clementines with the best flavour come from regions in which the night-time temperatures are fairly cool, relatively speaking. The Mediterranean island of Corsica has a climate that is ideally suited to the requirements of clementines: not too hot in summer with cool nights (12°C/54°F) in the autumn and winter. In other regions, in which the night-time temperatures do not drop, the clementines are picked while they are green and placed in ripening chambers to bring out their colour. A similar method is used for mandarins, although unfortunately, they are very difficult to come by nowadays. The reason for this is that it is not possible to cultivate mandarins without pips. The consumer demands pipless fruit, so the clementine has replaced this fruit with its typical and perhaps most delicious flavour of all citrus fruits. You should be able to get hold of satsumas or other varieties of mandarins. The flavour is very similar to that of the ordinary mandarin and it is very rich in juice (see p. 40-41).

The lime

The lime that originates from Malaysia is becoming increasingly popular in Europe. Its green colour is due to the fact that temperatures never drop below 15°C (59°F) in the countries of origin. Limes contain more juice than lemons but less vitamin C.

The fruit of the calamondin orange makes delicious marmalade.

A particularly unusual cultivar is the Combava from the island of Reunion. Limes with their fresh taste are suitable above all for cocktails. You can also preserve the fruit and make jam out of it. In the USA and Britain it is used to make pies and decorate cakes, and makes a delicious garnish for fish such as salmon and tuna. (see p. 36).

The grapefruit

The grapefruit comes from Florida and has a more defined flavour than the pampelmousse. It is particularly low in calories, so perhaps that explains its popularity. For some years now, particularly mild varieties have been available, these have rosy coloured flesh, like the 'Star Ruby' variety (see p. 38).

The citron

Citrons were once of great culinary importance, as they were processed to make candied fruit peel or citronate. Nowadays, the area given over to cultivating the citron has been drastically reduced in Europe as the manufacture of candied fruits is time-consuming and expensive (see p. 37).

Things to know about citrus plants

Uses in medicine and in perfume manufacturing

Citrus plants are not confined to culinary uses. They play an important part in the extraction of etheric oils for use in medicine and for perfume manufacture, where differing citrus species and varieties yield oils with specific qualities.

Healing oils

Oils are produced from the peel, the leaves and the flowers of different citrus species. Bergamot oil is obtained through cold pressing the wafer thin peel of the bergamot orange. It was traditionally used in Italian folk medicine for the control of high temperatures in the sick. In addition to this, the Italian doctor Paolo Rosvesti found during his research that the reviving qualities of bergamot oil make it effective in the treatment of depressive complaints.
Neroli oil is produced by distilling bitter orange flowers and it has a sweet heavy scent. It was named after the Italian Countess of Nerola who used the oil extensively. As do most etheric oils extracted from citrus plants, it has a calming, soothing effect on the nervous system and is especially good in combatting sleep disturbances and anxiety/panic attacks.
Petit grain oil is derived from the leaves and twigs of the bitter orange and has a similar effect to that of Neroli oil. Etheric oils from citrus plants are also frequently used in aromatherapy. Etheric oils can also be evaporated and inhaled by means of a scented lamp.

Perfumes

Etheric citrus oils are a basic ingredient in the manufacture of perfumes. A famous example is Eau de Cologne that derives its fresh scent and reviving effect from the etheric oils of bergamot and lemon. It was created by an Italian immigrant to Cologne during the last century. Neroli, one of the most beautiful scents, is the basic ingredient of many great perfumes. Generally speaking, all eaux de toilette that contain etheric citrus oils have an extremely refreshing quality. Not only the Europeans, but also the Native Americans in the rainforests of Brazil have been manufacturing wonderfully fresh and herby perfumes for generations according to ancient recipes based on lemons and mandarins. These perfumes are now sent to Europe as genuine natural products.
The scents of the leaves and flowers mean that a lover of citrus plants will be doubly spoiled. With a little practise, you will quickly become a specialist and will be able to distinguish between the sweetish heavy perfume of orange and calamondin flowers, the sweet, fresh scent of lemon and citron flowers and the more savory, green scents of bitter oranges, grapefruits or mandarin leaves.

My tip: Even rubbing the back of your hand vigorously across the leaves (care should be taken with thornier varieties like bitter orange and citron) will be sufficient to coax the wonderful scent out of the cells on the surface of the leaves.
If you are travelling around the Mediterranean, take a break from the beaches and go on a trip to a citrus plantation. Under the intense heat of the sun, a very individual, scent laden climate is created. In the 19th century the French writer Alphonse Daudet reported on his travels: "To really get to know orange trees, you have to see them in the countries where they grow naturally, on the Balearic islands, Sardinia, Corsica, in Algeria, in the golden blue air, the sultry warm atmosphere of the Mediterranean regions..."

Etheric oils with specific qualities are extracted from the leaves, flowers and peel of the various citrus plants. They are used in medicine as healing oils and are the basic ingredient in perfume manufacture.

Choosing and arranging

You can create a Mediterranean atmosphere on your balcony or patio with just a few citrus plants. To achieve the desired effect you need to consider a few important criteria when buying your plants and choosing a position for them.

The instructions on the following pages are intended to help you plant your citrus trees, choose the the right containers and also choose exactly the right setting for them.

Left: Seating areas are perfect places for citrus plants – here a kumquat is combined with various Mediterranean plants.

Above: Clementine 'Corsica' takes its name from the island where it is the most cultivated variety.

Position, buying and planting

Conditions on site

Citrus plants are more robust and less demanding than is generally assumed, however, requirements do vary considerably from species to species. The mini-climate created in the position they are to be kept, will be more or less favourable depending on how closely it matches the climatic conditions in places where citrus plants naturally grow (mild winters, not too hot or dry summers). The lemon, for example, originates from a region between the Himalayas, northern Burma and south China – a region with a temperate climate. It will, therefore, react sensitively to the cold but also to too much heat. The lime, on the other hand, originates from Malaysia and is a purely tropical plant that is extremely sensitive to the cold. The following growing conditions apply to ensure that citrus plants thrive on patios and balconies.

The position

Patios and balconies in a south-facing position are, of course, ideal. A patio surrounded by walls or a larger inner courtyard will create a particularly favourable mini-climate as the walls will store heat during the daytime and release it again during the night. East and west

facing positions will still be alright provided they are well protected against the wind. North-facing positions or very shady ones are out of the question for growing citrus plants.

Light

Citrus plants require absolutely direct sunlight and should be placed in a sunny, airy position for the summer. Plants that have spent the winter in overwintering quarters with poor light will gradually have to get used to the more intense radiation. They should be stood in semi-shade for the first fortnight or at least be well protected with some kind of shield during the midday hours. This also applies to plants that were bought in the spring and have fresh shoots.
Note: Always avoid placing citrus plants too close together, as they will create too much shade for each other with their dense foliage.

Protection from the wind

Citrus plants like it to be airy but are very sensitive to the wind and cannot stand draughts. They should, therefore, be well protected in windy and draughty positions. If they are not given shelter from the wind they will react by losing their leaves, turning bare and becoming

susceptible to waterlogging, pests and diseases. To protect your plants from the wind, use a wooden espalier or grid on your balcony or patio. This can be used to train climbing plants on every year and will provide shelter. A dense background full of constrasts will be created by evergreen ivy (*Hedera helix*), for example, with its dark green, shiny leaves or the *Parthenocissus tricuspidata* that will decorate your seating area with dark red foliage in the autumn when you have moved the citrus plants inside.

Water

When the temperature is high (midday), the stomata (slitted openings) on the undersides of the leaves close to prevent the plant from losing too much water through evaporation. If you water during the hottest part of the day there is a danger that the rootstock will become soaked and the roots will suffer the effects of waterlogging in spite of the dry climate. Water only in the morning or early evening. The most important thing is that citrus plants are watered regularly. Humidity of 60 per cent is optimal for citrus plants and some summer rain to prevent dirt from collecting on their leaves makes them feel particularly well.
If the air is dry and warm you can

Kumquats thrive in any sunny position.

without the protective blanket of soil. The exception is *Poncirus trifoliata* which is hardy outdoors in the UK (and many areas of the USA). It can cope with very short periods of frost and can survive brief exposure to temperatures as low as -30°C (-25°F). Generally speaking, though, temperatures should never drop to below 5-6°C (40-43°F) (see Overwintering, p. 55). The plant will cease growing at a temperature of 12°C (54°F). The temperatures should not, however, be allowed to climb beyond 30°C (85°F), as the plants will stop growing in the heat, too. From 13°C (56°F) upwards, growth will commence again. This temperature in the spring allows shoots to form. Temperatures of 0°C (32°F) are alright for the kumquat (*Fortunella japonica, F. margarita*).
Bitter orange can cope with 5°C (40°F), as can the mandarin (*C. reticulata*), and orange (*C. sinensis*).
10°C (50°F) is bearable for calamondin orange (X *Citrofortunella microcarpa*), lime (*C. aurantiifolia*), pampelmousse (*C. maxima*), citron (*C. medica*) and grapefruit (*C. x paradisi*).

Important: Never stand your citrus plants outside until after the last cold snap in spring, as frosts in late May can lead to the young shoots freezing to death.

increase the humidity by gently spraying the plants with some lime-free water.

Important: Do not spray in direct sunlight as the little droplets that remain on the leaves react like tiny magnifying glasses and can lead to dreadful burns. These burns can be recognized as round to oval, light brown spots.

Temperature

The optimal growing conditions for citrus plants lie in a temperature range of 20-30°C (69-85°F). All citrus plants are very sensitive to the cold and will suffer even at 4-5°C (38-40°F). In addition, growing these plants in large containers means they are more susceptible to the cold as the plants have to make do

Position, buying and planting

Where to buy citrus plants

Large garden centres buy citrus plants directly from the South, obtain them from specialist wholesalers or may even propagate their own Mediterranean plants. The specialist staff will be trained and you will, in some instances, be able to obtain regular care certificates. In any case, ask for information on plants and growing them as well as for the relevant accessories. Alternatively, you should be able to obtain citrus plants by mail order from specialist growers – these are listed in the *RHS Plant Finder*. If you are buying in spring it may be worth trying some of the larger flower shops in your area. Many stock a wide selection of citrus plants once the weather is warm enough for them to be displayed outside. Florists are highly skilled at grouping container plants together so you should be able to find unusual and decorative specimens in attractive containers and will, at the same time, be inspired by the different decorative ideas for balcony or patio plants.

Fruit-bearing plants should be transported with great care.

When to buy citrus plants

Citrus plants are, of course, available all the year round but the main sale times are in the spring and the autumn. While most citrus plants are in their flowering stage in the spring, by June and the beginning of July, you will be able to obtain plants with small, green fruits.

My tip: Purchasing in spring is, of course, recommended so that you can enjoy the plants on your patio or balcony during the summer months. Buy your plants with fruit already present as the chances of harvesting them that same year will be much higher.

Choosing and buying

In the autumn, there will be another large selection that will not, however, include as many varieties as in the spring. In October when citrus plants are taken indoors in northern latitudes, the main season for citrus fruit is just beginning in the Mediterranean area. Now the plants are laden with fruit that may be partially coloured due to the first cooler night-time temperatures. Should you be in possession of a winter garden with cooler temperatures (not over 16°C (61°F) or another brighter, cooler position, you should look-out for clementine, mandarin or orange trees. Citrus plants that do not yet display any evidence of flowers will still look wonderful as green plants. Another advantage is that the prices of green citrus plants will be well below those of flowering specimens.

What to watch for when purchasing

There are no reliable quality standards for citrus plants. The trading value will be determined by the general quality: a healthy plant, harmonious shape and growth, vigorous green foliage with secondary shoots and the presence of flowers and fruits, with the latter determining the price. Watch for the following when choosing and buying:

● The shape of the plant should be harmonious - that means, the proportions between the pot, the stem and the crown should work out with a ratio of ⅓: ⅓: ⅓. In the case of box-tree shapes, the pot should have a ratio of ⅓:⅔ with the plant. We do not recommend miniature plants in giant pots because the roots will become poorly distributed. A bush should branch properly and the crown of a semi-standard citrus plant should be round.

● Shoots that have followed on from the last pruning should be well visible. Too many cut surfaces with bud formations that have not progressed very far indicate pruning at the last minute (while preparing for delivery) which will lead to weakening of the plant.

● The stem should be smooth, the base of the main shoots should look healthy and have a greyish green colour.

● The grafting point should be clean and have grown well together (swellings, loose bark or accumulations of oozing resin indicate disease).

● The foliage should be a fresh green and not display any yellowing (a sign of nutrient deficiency or fungal infection).

● The plant should be well rooted. Test this by carefully holding the plant at the bottom end of the stem and moving it about gently. If the movement is too easy and it feels loose, rooting will not be good.

● Ask a member of the garden centre or shop staff to inspect the rootstock, as it should look well rooted with healthy, light-coloured roots.

Transportation

Citrus plants should, if possible, be transported upright or at most lying diagonally. The pot and the rootstock should be stood on a supportive base so the plant cannot roll about or branches be broken off. Protect the surface of the pot with a layer of newspaper so the soil/compost cannot fall out. Plants that are flowering or bear small fruits are sensitive and will have to be transported with great care. Make absolutely sure that there are no leaf burns if the plant is transported close to a window in your car. This is especially important in summer, as burns can appear in just a few minutes. We recommend wrapping the plant with a light cloth or white paper even if it is only going to be a short journey.

Choose a container to match the size and shape of your citrus plant.

Plant compost

The compost for large container plants should be particularly rich in nutrients and humus. It also needs to be porous as citrus plants consume a great deal of water. A mixture of ¼ ericaceous compost, ½ compost and ¼ sand will most readily meet their requirements. The addition of ericaceous compost creates a slightly acid medium, the compost supplies a high content of humus and nutrients, the sand (or similar substance, see pp. 26/27) enables the roots to obtain an adequate supply of oxygen.

When should they be repotted?

Citrus plants should only be repotted when the rootstock is well equipped with roots. The best time to do this is usually before the first shoots appear at the beginning of the year – depending on cultivation conditions, that is the months of February to May in the northern hemisphere. Ornamental plants can, as a rule, remain in the same pot for 1-2 years. They can be repotted every 3 years. Once the plant has attained a size where it can no longer be repotted (for example, a 3 m (10 ft) tall lemon tree), you should freshen up the surface of the compost every spring. Then

every 5-6 years you should change the compost altogether. If the tree is more than 20 years old, you should change the compost every 10-15 years. To do this, either remove the pot, or in the case of Versailles containers, remove the sides and carefully pick off the outer layer of compost. Then repot the tree again with fresh compost in the same container.

Note: Guarantee optimal growth in younger trees by ensuring that the new pot is not too large and the diameter is no more than 4-10 cm (1½-4 in) wider than that of the old pot.

Planting containers

If they are to have a long life, container plants need containers that will ensure their wellbeing (see pp. 30-31). The container should be selected carefully to suit the chosen citrus plant, taking into account its quality, shape and value. Fully grown lemon trees are best planted in a durable container (for example, an oak trough). Citrus trees that can cope with short-term frost like the 'Meyer' lemon or even longer periods of frost, like the Japanese bitter orange, should be planted in frost-proof containers (large wooden containers, pots by English Whichford pottery and to a limited extent also Impruneta terracotta).

Note: Industrially manufactured terracotta containers or troughs are, as a rule, not frost-proof.

Drainage is very important. A plant trough should always have a means for allowing water to drain away. Terracotta containers usually have holes in the bottom. In the case of Versailles containers, the smaller models have a galvanized, perforated metal floor, the larger ones have a grid above the bottom. Plant containers with a water reservoir should not be used due to the risk of waterlogging.

Important: Smaller pots that are set in secondary pots run the risk of collecting rainwater etc. and this should always be poured away. The secondary pot can be set on small feet (you can use bricks for this) to improve the drainage of excess water and ventilation of the plant. The depth of the container is a deciding factor. It should be suited to the type of root of the plant: for shallow-rooting types, a normal or slightly more shallow pot will be alright. Small calamondin bushes can easily be planted in basins. A tall container will be essential for bitter orange trees or varieties grafted on to them as, unlike all other citrus trees, these have a long tap root.

Planting citrus plants

1 First place a drainage layer of crushed lava rock or Hortag granules in the bottom of a Versailles container.

The cultivation of citrus plants in containers requires two planting procedures. First, the young plants are pricked out and potted in the first proper container. The repotting of medium to large specimens usually occurs after that in a cycle of three years. In the case of very large, tree-like citrus plants that are already growing in a large container, it will be sufficient to freshen up the surface of the compost once a year.

Potting and repotting young plants
Illustrations 2 to 5

First, prepare the pot that is intended for the citrus plant. Clay pots should be soaked in water before use so the walls of the pot do not absorb moisture from the compost. Then fill the bottom with a 2-4 cm (¾ -1½ in) thick drainage layer of

granulated lava rock, or Hortag (see illustration 2). In the case of troughs with a capacity of several litres and large drainage holes at the bottom, the holes should be covered beforehand with a curved crock. Afterwards, fill the pot up with part of the compost. Now, carefully loosen the plant out of its old pot and check the rootstock for density of roots. To do this, carefully lay a hand on the surface of the rootstock so the plant stem is between your forefinger and middle finger (see illustration 3). Then lightly tap the pot on the edge of a table to loosen the rootstock from the edge of the pot and you will be able to lift it out quite easily. If you can see at least 3-4 roots on the surface of the rootstock, the young plant can be repotted immediately. In the case of older specimens that are ready for repotting, the rootstock will often have a densely matted

root system growing through it. Here, carefully use your fingers to loosen the mass gently without damaging any of the roots (see illustration 4). Now stand the rootstock on the ready prepared drainage layer in the new pot and shake in more compost with the other hand. Firmly press down the compost around the edge of the pot and more carefully in the area of the neck of the root (see illustration 5). The plant should sit firmly in the new pot. The stem should not move when tapped.

Important: In all cases,

leave an edge for watering (corresponding to the height of the marked edge of the pot) and water thoroughly once. During this initial watering, the rootstock and the new compost should be very moist.

Planting in Versailles containers
Illustration 1

First fill the bottom of the wooden trough with a drainage layer of lava granules, Hortag, or crocks and place a thin layer of compost on top.

Now set the plant with

its rootstock in the pot and fill up with compost in several stages. Each time, press the compost down into the corners of the container with a piece of wooden stick and press the compost down more carefully with your hands around the neck of the root.

Freshening up the compost

After clearing large containers out of their winter quarters, freshen up the compost. To do this, carefully remove the top layer of compost – depending on the size of the pot, to a depth of 5-15 cm (2-6 in). Then slightly loosen the surface of the compost and fill it up with fresh compost. At the same time, organic fertilizer can be added (see Care, p. 45).

My tip: A mini-rake makes it easier to loosen the surface of the compost and allows better ventilation of the compost.

The compost

Nearly all citrus plants love a slightly acid compost (pH factor 5.5-6.5) that is rich in organic substances (humus). The sour orange (*Citrus aurantium*) is an exception as it will adapt to all types of acidity and will grow well in less acid conditions (pH factor 6.5-7) as will the myrtle-leaved variety (*Citrus aurantium var. myrtifolia*) and any Citrus cultivar grafted onto *Citrus aurantium* rootstock.

My tip: Some garden centres and specialist suppliers may even be able to provide you with a special mixture for citrus plants. A plant or tree nursery that specializes in Mediterranean plants and especially in citrus plants will certainly mix a compost up for you according to the recipe on page 23.

The drainage layer

The drainage layer should never be missing, as citrus plants react extremely sensitively to waterlogging that is most often caused by lack of ventilation in the root area. Plant roots not only need water – without oxygen they can neither absorb nutrients nor carry out their normal metabolic processes. A drainage layer is, therefore, an additional protection against lack of oxygen. The most suitable substances are granulated lava rock, Hortag, clay or broken up pot fragments.

2 Place a 2-4 cm (¾-1½ in) thick drainage layer in the bottom of the pot.

3 Loosen the plant and, supporting rootstock, remove from the pot.

4 Gently loosen the rootstock around the outer surface.

5 Press down the compost, carefully around the neck of root.

Position, buying and planting

Designing with citrus plants

Citrus plants lend patios and balconies something of the flair and intimacy of the typical inner courtyards built in the centre of Mediterranean houses. There are no rules or limits when you are designing Mediterranean-style surroundings: from severely classical (in the style of Versailles) to natural (a little piece of Tuscany) through to a free design with your own choice of accessories, there are endless possibilities. You will have your own ideas but for many people, citrus plants help to create a bit of a holiday dream without ever having to leave their own patios.

Mediterranean flair on your patio or balcony

A patio is a place where inside and outside worlds meet. It is both a living area and part of the garden and is a popular area for family and friends to relax. Sunny seating areas are ideal places for citrus plants. Here, they will be in full view, and their evergreen foliage and intense perfume will prove great attractions. When designing the area, you should always choose small, medium and large plants that can either be placed together as a group or beside each other to form a "green wall". Espaliers are also eminently suitable for framing a

sitting area and have a particularly attractive effect.

You can also conjure up a bit of the South on your balcony. Where space is limited the balcony can be made to appear bigger if plant boxes and hanging containers are attached to the railing or wall. Scented plants, for example, can be combined in these containers with citrus plants. One ideal solution is to plant citrus espaliers in narrow boxes along the housewall. The warmth absorbed by the wall and then reflected is particularly encouraging for fruit formation.

A few specialities

Among the many citrus species that are generally extremely sensitive to cold, there is one frost-hardy variety, the Japanese bitter orange (*Poncirus trifoliata*). Nevertheless, even this variety should be given a sheltered position, for example, in front of a south-facing wall. The plant will still be very attractive, in spite of losing its leaves in the winter and having a rather bizarre shape of growth. The flowers appear in the spring and transform the bush into a white cloud of scent. Even more unusual in its shape of growth is a cultivar of *Poncirus trifoliata*, called the 'Flying Dragon'. It is particularly noted for its zig-zag

shaped branches, but grows very slowly. Even though these two cultivars of citrus plant are very decorative, one thing should be considered: both have long, sharp thorns. You should take great care that children do not get too close to them.

Combining large and small

In order to capture the atmosphere of scented citrus gardens, a certain volume of foliage needs to be created. It is definitely a good idea to choose an attractive combination of small and large leafed varieties, regularly branching and stiffly growing plants, bushes and espaliers or tree-like citrus plants. Among the small-leafed varieties are, for example, mandarin, clementine or calamondin oranges in a bush form or quarter stem form. An interesting contrast can then be formed with large-leafed varieties like bitter orange, grapefruit and lemons.

This patio brimming with Mediterranean plants creates the illusion of a southern courtyard.

Decorative pots can be used to help set the Mediterranean scene.

Orange trees also have large leaves and regular branching, while lemons, citron (*Citrus medica*) and pampelmousse (*Citrus maxima*) with their fairly stiff looking, individual shapes make an unusual sight.

You can create a very attractive group using just three different citrus plants. For example, a lemon bush, a calamondin orange as a quarter size tree and a half-size bitter orange tree. Even a single citrus plant can look beautiful if it is in good condition and displayed in a suitably decorative container, for example, in a handmade terracotta pot from Tuscany.

Arrangements with other flowering plants

Citrus plants come from the sunny Mediterranean where brightness dominates. Brilliant white and glowing blue should not, therefore, be missing in any flower arrangement. Mix together white flowers (for example, large daisies, petunias, geraniums, hortensia, *Impatiens*

New-Guinea, oleander, *Datura, Bacopa*) with blue flowers (for example, lavender, *Plumbago*, ornamental lilies, hortensia). For typically Mediterranean plant arrangements choose: oleander, myrtle, olive tree, bay laurel, box, bougainvillea, callistemon, hibiscus, *Lantana* and a selection of Mediterranean herbs such as rosemary, lavender, cotton lavender, and thyme.

The matching plant container

Plant containers should be chosen to round off the shapes and lines of the total design. Citrus plants and plant containers should be well matched and create a harmonious overall impression. They should always form a complete unit and complement each other.

Traditional containers for ornamental citrus plants are handmade terracotta pots from Tuscany, Versaille wooden containers, and noble *Anduze* vases from the Cevennes in southern France. The terracotta products that originate from Impruneta near Florence are particularly beautiful. Handmade and fired for up to 48 hours at 1000°C (1832°F), they are much admired for their typical whitish patina. Thanks to their extreme hardness they are also generally frost-proof.

Note: There are no one hundred per cent frost-proof terracotta vessels. One exception is the unique pottery created in the Victorian style by the English Whichford Pottery, that comes supplied with a ten year frost guarantee. Industrially produced terracotta pots are often very porous and crack easily in frosty temperatures.

The Versailles containers (see illustration p. 26) were designed especially for orange trees at the court of Louis XIV in the 17th century. These oakwood boxes, left in their natural colour or varnished white or light green, come in different sizes (50-130 cm/ 20-52 in). They are equipped with solid cast iron hinges and can be taken apart. This makes it easier to transport them and allows a citrus plant to be kept in the same container for years. Nowadays there are very few manufacturers who will build them according to the traditional specifications. The specialist trade does however stock numerous imitations that are considerably cheaper.

The *Anduze vase* (30-100 cm/ 12-40 in tall) was created by a potter in the Cevennes in 1610 according to models of the tulip shaped Medici vase. Its typical flame pattern and ocre-yellow colour is due to the type of clay found in this region. A high quality glaze, a handmade

curving base and the delicate ornaments laid on the rim make these vases very handsome and noble. They were used for decoration in the Versailles orangery and are still, considered to be the classic shape of containers for ornamental citrus plants. Any attractively shaped wooden container made of oak or chestnut is suitable. Even rustic baskets may make attractive secondary pots. Baskets made from olive branches with their typical grey-green colour are extremely attractive.

Decoration

Try to include the contrasting shades of white and blue in your choice of accessories. There are so many decorative objects that could be included as part of a Mediterranean setting. Numerous pottery products, as well as ceramic, porcelain and glass can help to set the scene. A deep blue fruit bowl or a lemonade jug with matching glasses will bring the typical Mediterranean colours into the picture. Many wonderful materials and fabrics are available for cushions and tablecloths in your seating area. Look for typically southern patterns, for example, Provençal designs. Colourful tiles on the floor of your balcony or patio will complete the look.

Oranges are not the only fruit

From the orange to the grapefruit – the range of citrus plants is large and the multitudes of species and varieties are almost too many to grasp. Yellow and orange coloured, large and small fruits, well-known and unusual – the following chapter will introduce you to the most suitable species for your balcony and patio and help you to make all the right choices.

Left: Large and small, yellow or orange coloured fruits, green and variegated foliage and delicate flowers – these are the contrasts which make citrus plants so attractive.

Above: Deep-blue Tibouchina urvilleana *forms a wonderful contrast to the sunny yellow citrus fruits.*

The most popular citrus plants

The most beautiful citrus plants for your balcony and patio

Deep green, shiny leaves, scented flowers and glowing fruits – citrus plants have a beauty and charm of their own. The choice of species and varieties is almost limitless, and numerous species are suitable for growing in large containers. The following selection is intended as a simple step-by-step guide to the fascinating and complex world of citrus plants.

Large and small fruits

The following overview of the different species divided into yellow and orange coloured fruits, and an introduction to the various sizes of fruit – from 'maxi' to 'mini' – should help you to pinpoint the well-known varieties and discover some rare ones that you may not have encountered before.

First, we introduce the lemon and other green to yellow lemon-like plants with the more acid tasting fruits. Next, we look at oranges and the other citrus plants bearing orange coloured fruits with their sweet to bitter-sweet flavours.

The selection and categories of fruits chosen here will also give an idea of the variations in shapes and sizes of citrus fruits. The largest fruits, citrons, may weigh up to 2 kg (4½ lb) and grapefruits with a diameter of 25 cm (10 in) are not rare. They are followed by medium sized ones (mandarins and clementines) and finally the small fruits (calamondin oranges and kumquats).

Tips on care and design

The species and varieties mentioned here can be obtained in the gardening trade and are all, without exception, suitable for growing in large containers. In the case of the bitter orange, the tradition of growing it in containers has a long history, as the hundred-year old specimens in orangeries prove. Newer cultivars, for example the limequat, are also ideally suited for growing in containers on balconies and patios. This is thanks to improvements in research institutes and specialized citrus plant nurseries in Tuscany and Corsica. The plants listed here will also produce fruit when grown in containers under optimal conditions – some less easily, like the grapefruit, others extremely abundantly like the 'chinotto' (a cultivar of *Citrus aurantium*) or the calamondin orange. Not all species have the same requirements so relevant instructions on care are given in the individual plant profiles. For example, if you want to harvest ripe fruit of the grapefruit, they should, if possible be grown in a greenhouse or conservatory. The calamondin orange, on the other hand, will adapt to nearly all situations. The Japanese bitter orange can even cope with days of frost and will also make do with a cold and not very bright room as winter quarters.

My tip: Try your luck with a calamondin orange. It will overwinter without any problems in heated living rooms and can be kept inside all year round if your balcony should turn out to be in an unfavourable position.

Tips on uses

Nearly all the citrus plants shown and described here belong to the group of agrumen, that is, of edible citrus fruits. Edible does not, however, mean that a fruit can necessarily be eaten raw. Sometimes, a delicious dish is created only through a certain method of preparation, for example, by turning calamondin oranges into marmalade or the well-known English bitter orange marmalade that is made out of the fruit of bitter oranges.

Lemon
Citrus limon

Originally a native of China, the lemon was introduced and distributed throughout the Mediterranean area by the Arabs from about 1100 AD. *Citrus limon* 'Eureka' is the best known of the many cultivars; it was first propagated in California in 1858 from seed originating in Italy. In southern France it is called the "four seasons lemon" as it flowers all year round and constantly produces new fruit.

Appearance: As an ornamental plant it has a bush-like shape. It is particularly attractive due to the flowers and fruit appearing at the same time. The purple tinged white flowers have a strong scent. The large fruit has a yellow, thick peel.

Care: There are two possibilities of overwintering: 1. In a cool room in the house, with the following basic rules: the warmer the room is, the brighter it should be; the plant should be stood right beside the window in a permanently heated room. Lack of light will result in yellowing or falling of individual leaves. Vigorous pruning in the spring before the plant begins to shoot will help it to produce new healthy growth.
2. In a cool (5–10°C/ 40–50°F), if necessary dark room. Reduce watering drastically, but avoid complete drying out of the rootstock. Here, increased falling of leaves due to lack of light is normal. Prune back in the spring. After the last cold snap in spring, remove it from its winter quarters. Let it get used to sunlight again gradually and water regularly but sparingly. Fertilize weekly. Frequently cut into shape.

Design: Due to its all-year round flowering and fruiting, it is best used as a solitary plant, a bush or espalier in the Tuscan style. The first fruits on espaliers will be particularly good, due to better light conditions.

Warning: The plant has thorns! Stand it in a position where it will not present any risk to young children.

Lemon (Citrus limon).

Lemon and lime

Lemon 'Meyer' (Citrus limon x sinensis).

Lime (Citrus aurantiifolia).

Lemon 'Meyer'
Citrus limon x sinensis

This species was introduced to the USA from China in 1908 by the explorer Meyer and is thought to be a hybrid of the lemon and the orange.

Appearance: Compact growth. Flowers all year, with the main flowering time in the spring. The juicy, mild tasting fruit is smaller than that of the lemon and has a thin peel with an orange-yellow colour.

Care: Relatively easy and straightforward, it is more robust than the lemon. In milder regions, overwintering may be possible on a balcony or patio. This plant is very hardy with respect to climate and may even cope with a few hours of frost to -5°C/23°F). Otherwise keep in a cool (5-8°C/40-46°F), bright room. It will react to lack of light relatively rapidly by increased loss of leaves. Pruning back before the shoots appear in the spring is recommended.

Design: Ideal as a solitary bush because of its compact growth.

Lime
Citrus aurantiifolia

The lime originated from Malaysia and came across to Europe via India and Persia.

Appearance: Small tree or bush with irregular branches equipped with sharp thorns. The small leaves are light green and the flowers are white with a purple tinge. The acidic lime produces green or light yellow fruits that have a firm flesh. The fruits can be large or small. *Citrus aurantiifolia* 'Tahiti' is related to the lime. Its fruit is pipless and has a very thin peel. Among the sweet limes are *Citrus limetta* and *Citrus limettoides* which bear yellow fruit with very mild-tasting flesh.

Care: This citrus plant is the most sensitive of all to the cold. Temperatures should not be too cool (10°C/50°F) and overwinter in a bright place. It will grow only slowly and will start producing shoots as soon as it gets warm.

Uses: The basic ingredient for soft drinks is derived from lime juice in the USA.

Citron (Citrus medica).

Bergamot (Citrus x bergamia).

Citron
Citrus medica

The citron is the oldest cultivated citrus plant and arrived in the Mediterranean area in antiquity via Persia.
Appearance: Bush-shaped plant with long, tough thorns and often pointed, oval leaves. Flowers are white, purplish in bud. Enormous fruit with thick, irregular green peel that gradually turns yellow during ripening.
Care: This plant requires lots of nutrients so will need a plentiful supply of organic fertilizer. Do not stand it too close to other plants as it needs to be able to get sufficient light Overwintering at about 10°C (50°F) in a bright position. Fairly sensitive to the cold so plants should be taken indoors at the end of the first month of autumn.
Uses: Processing into candied fruit/peel. *Citronate*, or candied peel, is produced from the peel and is used in baking and for desserts.

Bergamot
Citrus x bergamia

The bergamot is a native of China and India and represents a natural cross between the bitter orange (*Citrus aurantium*) and the lime (*Citrus aurantiifolia*). It is believed to have been cultivated in Italy as early as 1700. In Calabria, the bergamot was cultivated for the production of bergamot oil that is a basic ingredient in the manufacture of perfume. The oil is found in the peel which is pared away finely and pressed to release the oil.
Appearance: The pear-shaped fruit has a thick, yellow skin, a characteristic scent and tastes sour.
Care: As for the citron.
Design: Bergamot is a rarity as an ornamental citrus plant that owes its attractive effect to its unusual fruit. Ideally it should be placed near a seating area so its particularly fresh scent can be enjoyed.

Grapefruit and pampelmousse

Grapefruit
Citrus x paradisi

Originates from the Antilles and introduced to Florida in 1814.

Appearance: This fast-growing, spreading plant has quite large flowers. The yellow fruit with an average diameter of 15 cm (6 in) has light yellow flesh which has a small amount of acid.

Care: Requires plenty of room. To ensure you will obtain ripe fruit you need to 'thin' the fruit. The first fruit, after flowering, should be reduced to at most one or two pieces. Select them, if possible, near the centre of the tree, close to the stem. Ripening of the fruit will take up to a year. In the summer feed twice with organic fertilizer. Do not overwinter in too cool conditions, if possible in a greenhouse or winter garden (10-12°C/50-54°F). The variety 'Lipo' can be overwintered at slightly cooler temperatures (to 5°C/40°F).

Design: The variety 'Lipo' from Tuscany is particularly suitable for patios and balconies

Grapefruit (Citrus paradisi).

and is a hybrid of the lemon and the grapefruit. It has a low growth and flowers all year round.

Pampelmousse
Citrus maxima

The pampelmousse, or pomelo, and the grapefruit are closely related but belong to two different species.

Appearance: The young shoots thickly covered in fluffy hairs are typical for the plant. The very large fruit (with a diameter of 25 cm/ 10 in) has yellow to pink coloured flesh.

Care: As for grapefruit.

Left: Pampelmousse *(Citrus maxima)*

Orange
Citrus sinensis

The orange originates from China. Oranges can be sub-divided into navel, common and blood oranges.

Appearance: Beautiful, deep green foliage, some older specimens flower or produce fruit all year round.

Care: Shorten shoots that grow up fast immediately, in order to achieve a regularly shaped crown (see Pruning, pp. 48/49). Overwintering is best at 5°C (40°F), as bright as possible. Annually, after overwintering, place the plant in its usual position on the balcony or patio but change the side that faces the sun.

Design: The orange looks very elegant as a solitary plant in a Versailles container.

Orange (Citrus sinensis)

Bitter orange
Citrus aurantium

This species belongs to the oldest citrus plants growing in the Mediterranean.

Appearance: Attractive growth. Provided it flowers, it will often produce extremely large fruit in our climate.

Note: It carries long, tough thorns.

Care: Very adaptable with respect to soil and water quality (will cope with pH factor above 6.5). Pruning, see under the section on Oranges.

Citrus aurantium

Overwintering at 5-10°C (40-50°F), as bright as possible; more resistant to cold than the orange, it will even cope with temperatures below freezing for a few hours.

Design: The various different varieties are suitable for combining with each other.

Mandarins

Mandarin
Citrus reticulata

The mandarin originally came from China and Japan and was one of the last citrus fruits to reach the Mediterranean area of Algeria in about 1805. The common mandarin (*Citrus reticulata*) is the *real* mandarin from the Mediterranean area. There are many varieties, so mandarin fruits can vary tremendously. The mandarin 'Kara' (*Citrus reticulata* 'Kara') is a hybrid of the satsuma 'Owari' and the mandarin 'King'. It was created in California in 1915. This variety has very juicy, fine flesh.

Appearance: The mandarin tree is planted outside in plantations and grows up to 3m (9 ft) tall. The dark green, shiny leaves are narrow and longish, the white flowers have a very intense, heavy-sweet scent. The fruit is orange, its size and shape depend on the variety.

Care: From the last month of spring to the first month of autumn, stand it directly in the sun. The crown will rapidly gain in volume and the growth upwards will be particularly vigorous. This requires regular cutting back of shoots (see, Pruning, pp. 48/49). Overwinter in cool (5°C (40°F) to maximum 10°C (50°F)) and bright conditions. Warm temperatures and lack of light will cause it to lose its leaves.

Citrus reticulata.

Mandarin (*Citrus reticulata*).

Uses: Citrus reticulata is probably the most beautiful of all citrus plants with respect to its scent and fruit flavour. It is the only plant with the typical mandarin flavour and scent. It is, unfortunately, becoming increasingly rare as, being a fruit that always has pips, it is being replaced on the market by clementines which seldom have pips. If you want to sample that fabulous mandarin scent, gently rub one of the leaves to release the etheric oils and its intense aroma.

Citrus reticulata 'Kara'.

Citrus 'Satsuma'.

Clementine 'Corsica'.

Satsuma

Citrus reticulata

The satsuma came into being through a mutation of the mandarin and originated in the Japanese province of Satsuma where it is cultivated in large quantities and processed into preserves and jam that are exported. In Europe, the season for citrus fruits begins in November with the arrival of satsumas. There are several cultivars: some are already ripe in September, others at the end of December and later. The main areas of cultivation are Spain and Morocco.

Appearance: The fruit is not round in shape but slightly flattened and mainly pipless. The skin is loose on the delicate, sour-sweet flesh and is easy to peel.

Care: As for the mandarin. Satsumas belong to the group of citrus plants that are most resistant to cold.

Design: A decorative variant is the *variegated satsuma* with its yellow green variegated leaves.

Clementine

Citrus reticulata

The clementine is a derivative of the mandarin and was discovered in 1906 by Pere Clement. It was probably a natural hybrid of the mandarin (*Citrus reticulata*) and the bitter orange (*Citrus aurantium*). The clementine 'Corsica' is a very beautiful variety with particularly good and plentiful fruit. It was created on the island of Corsica and is still the most cultivated variety in France today.

Appearance:
Clementine fruit ripens very early. Depending on the variety, the fruit can ripen from the middle of the second month of autumn. The colouring of the green peel can change to a strong shade of orange, as previously explained, through the cool night-time temperatures of around 12°C (54°F). In Corsica, this occurs from the middle of the last month of autumn. The fruits of clementines are mainly pipless.

Care: As for mandarins. Plenty of sun in summer.

Calamondin orange

Calamondin orange
Citrofortunella microcarpa

Originally came from South East Asia and is a hybrid of *Citrus reticulata* and *Fortunella species*. This species is known to us only as an ornamental citrus plant, while in Japan it is cultivated for the fruit. The fruit is inedible raw but can be processed to make candied fruit and marmalade.

Appearance: Calamondin orange trees are available in different sizes for pots right through to large container plants with heights of 2-3 m (6-9 ft). The intensely scented flowers renew themselves constantly. The fruit ripens easily and is a brilliant orange-red colour.

Calamondin orange (Citrofortunella microcarpa variegata).

Care: This is ideal for beginners as it is a very undemanding citrus plant. Overwintering is best in cool and bright positions at 5-8°C (40-46°F). If there are no overwintering quarters available, it can also be kept warm in the house or in a winter garden at a temperature of above 18°C (65°F). At these temperatures, however, the plant will continue growing so that constant, regular care will be necessary all year round (see Care, p. 45).

Design: The species most often cultivated in containers is x *Citrofortunella microcarpa* with green leaves (see right). A very decorative variety is x *Citrofortunella*

Calamondin orange

microcarpa variegata (above) which is noted for its attractive yellow green variegated leaves.

Uses: You can make marmalade out of fruit from your own harvest or cut them into segments to add to glasses of cool champagne or cocktails for drinking on long summer afternoons.

Kumquat
Fortunella sp.

The Latin name of this citrus plant was given to it by the British plant collector Robert Fortune, who discovered the plant in China in 1847 and brought it back to Europe. There are three varieties: *Fortunella japonica 'Marumi'* (with round fruit), *Fortunella margarita 'Nagami'* (with oval fruit) and *Fortunela x crassifolia 'Meiwa'* (with large round fruit). The limequat 'Eustis' (below right) is a hybrid created in Florida in 1909 out of *Citrus aurantiifolia* and *Fortunella sp*.

Appearance: The kumquat can be medium sized to a semi-tree shape. Its growth is slower than that of other citrus plants, so it is well suited to growing in containers. The leaves are elongated.

Care: Kumquats will thrive in any sunny position. Protect them well from parasites as the fruit will otherwise be inedible. Overwinter in a bright and cool place (at 5°C (40°F), the kumquat is resistant to cold and

Kumquat (Fortunella japonica).

will cope with temperatures around 0°C (32°F) for a few hours at a time.

Design: Kumquats are among the most attractive container plants. *F. margarita* with its oval, brilliant orange fruits makes a wonderful display. The limequat 'Eustis' is charming even as a young plant with its

Limequat 'Eustis'

small, yellow, durable fruit and is counted among the specialities of ornamental citrus plants.

Uses: The fruit is eaten with the peel intact. This is where the main sugar content is lodged and it provides an interesting contrast to the slightly bitter fruit flesh.

Flowers and fruits on citrus plants

Citrus plants are very robust plants in the wild. Hundred-year-old specimens in orangeries prove that they also thrive in large containers. By following exact instructions for their care, pruning and propagating, you will not only help your plants to produce healthy growth but you will also be able to propagate some species yourself.

Left: An attractive group of profusely fruiting citrus plants, including a dwarf bitter orange, a calamondin orange and an orange.

Above: Citrus plants and pinkish violet Bougainvillea glabra form an attractive combination.

Care of citrus plants

Correct watering

The water requirements of citrus plants depend on the size of the plant and the volume of its leaves, the temperature and the amount of sunlight.
Generally one can say:
● During the growth phase, water regularly and plentifully.
● Avoid waterlogging. Pour off the excess water that builds up in dishes or secondary pots.
● Use water that has been allowed to stand for a while and is free of lime.
Citrus plants have a high requirement of water on hot days and yet are sensitive to waterlogging. This means watering them sparingly but frequently so the rootstock can never dry out but is also never too moist. It is better to water too little than too much. Even if some leaf damage occurs due to the rootstock being too dry for a longer period (curling of leaves, dried up leaf tips), this is not dramatic compared to the risk of almost irreparable root rot caused by waterlogging.
My tip: If the rootstock does dry out on the odd occasion, stand the plant – if the size of the pot will allow – in a large container filled with temperate water so the rootstock can soak itself full of water from below. Afterwards, stand the plant for a while so the excess water is able to run off well from the pot. Large or heavy containers should be watered three or four times at intervals of a quarter of an hour.

Important: Citrus plants in clay pots need to be watered more often than plants in glazed containers or plastic pots, as more water is evaporated through the walls of clay pots.

The right way to fertilize

To keep your citrus plants healthy and growing well, you should work an organic fertilizer (guano, horn chips etc) into the compost at the beginning of the growth phase. Further doses of fertilizer will depend on the size and the condition of your plants.

Generally speaking:
● Put liquid fertilizer into the water once weekly (follow the instructions on the packet) from the end of spring until the beginning of autumn.
● Apply fertilizer to already moistened compost.
● In the winter months, fertilize only those varieties that never enter a rest period. Do this once a month.

Encouraging the formation of flowers

If your citrus plants do not appear to want to flower, the following methods can be used to stimulate flower formation:

Stress through dryness: Over a period of 2-3 weeks, gradually reduce the doses of water and finally cease watering altogether. After this period of dryness, water as before.
Special fertilizing: Treat plants that are unwilling to flower with a pure phosphorous fertilizer (bonemeal), twice at intervals of three weeks.

Encouraging the change of colour and size of fruit

The plants require cool night temperatures (around 16°C/61°F) so that the young formed fruit can colour properly. For this reason, clementines, for example, are not harvested until November in Corsica when the temperature at night has dropped sufficiently. If there is a great deal of fruit formation, the individual fruit will often remain small. Thin out some of the young fruit to obtain larger fruit, but do this while the fruit is still about pea-size.

The requirements of care for citrus plants vary. All species need plenty of water on hot days. In all cases, the following applies: water often in small doses, rather than too much at once, otherwise, there is a risk of waterlogging and root rot.

Pruning

Citrus plants should be kept in shape through regular pruning or they will form 'water sprouts'. These are vigorous shoots that deprive the plant of water and nutrients and rapidly shoot up above the normal height. Water sprouts may not flower for many years and when they develop fruit, begin to bend precariously downward. **Note:** Cut surfaces are very susceptible to diseases and it is important to work with a clean blade. Disinfect the blade before and after use by rubbing it down with alcohol or holding it in a flame.

root (illustration 1). The plant will fork at this point (see illustration 2). The height of the branching point will determine the final height of the stem. If you want to grow a tall stem, you should make the cut higher up.

Forming cut
Illustration 3

A citrus plant is particularly attractive with a shaped crown, and the round crown is characteristic (see illustration 3, curve indicated with dotted line). To do this, target the left side and cut off

3 The round crown is a characteristic feature of the shaping cut.

Formation of young plants
Illustrations 1 and 2

Young plants that have been raised from seed should be pruned in their second year, grafted young plants one year after grafting. Cut the plant below the third and fourth leaves above the neck of the

selected shoots. Use good sharp tree cutters. Finally, remove all further stray branches. Do not take any notice of flowers or fruits. The

1 Cut off the plant below the fourth leaf.

2 The plant will branch out from that point.

point where you cut should always lie above a leaf. The same aplies when you are cutting off shoots.
Cut out:
● The root suckers around the base of the plant.
● Where there are double shoots that run almost parallel upwards, cut off the inside shoot.
● Shoots that grow horizontally into the crown (cross shoots) and make it denser.
● Any weak shoots that hang downwards should be cut back to the base.

Important: Lemon and citron trees are naturally lanky and difficult to shape. With bush-like specimens, restrict yourself to thinning out the shoots and perform a light cutting back in the spring.

Cutting shoot tips
Illustration 4

This procedure involves cutting off the tip of a shoot that is growing faster than the other shoots. The tip includes the small leaves of the tip plus the two to four leaves below. Regularly cutting off shoot tips during the growth phase keeps the crown of the tree in shape. Not all shoot tips should be removed, however, as

4 The shoot tip is removed when pruning.

flowering would otherwise be prevented. Shorten the shoot tip by grasping it with forefinger and thumb above the leaf and pinching it off with your fingernails. This is known as 'wipping out'.
Important: Always remove the shoot tip above a leaf. If it is a side shoot, choose a leaf that points outwards.
My tip: If no flowers are growing on the shoot tips, you can use the shoot tip as a cutting.

Root suckers
Illustration 5

Root suckers from the rootstock occasionally grow on grafted citrus plants. They are situated at the base of the soil and grow very fast. Usually their leaves look different from those of the grafted part of the plant. As the wild shoots also require nutrients and water, they will interfere with the growth of the whole plant and should be systematically removed as early as possible and cut off at the base.

5 Root suckers sit on the base of the compost.

Radical cutting back
Illustration 6

There are cases when a radical cutting back is the last ditch means of healing a citrus plant. A lemon tree, for example, that has been overwintered in a room that was not sufficiently bright and too warm will react to these unfavourable conditions with increased loss of leaves. Cutting back will then be the only way to renew the plant and help

it to grow healthy shoots. Cut the plant back by about half and try at the same time to bring the crown into shape. The best time to do this is in the spring, before a new growth spurt begins.

6 The plant is cut right back by about half.

Care of citrus plants

Propagating citrus plants

Citrus plants belong to the more valuable and therefore more expensive large container plants and large specimens can cost a lot. If you do not wish to spend such a lot of money, the best idea is to propagate the plants from seed by yourself but you will have to wait a while until the plants are big enough. This method has the advantage that the plants will be used to their climate and position right from the beginning and will not need time to adapt or acclimatize. Citrus plants can be propagated in several different ways: from seed, from cuttings and through grafting. The latter is the most commonly used propagation method for citrus plants. Grafting and cuttings produce strong plants identical to the parent plant and better adapted to its position.

Grafting is the most frequent propagation method for citrus plants.

The tools

Whether you want several plants of one variety or have discovered an interesting plant during your holidays, provided you observe some basic rules, you should be able to propagate your citrus plants successfully.

The following utensils and tools will be required for propagating citrus plants:

● Seeding compost or or a type of compost suitable for growing young seedlings.

● Seed trays or pricking out boxes with a cover, or a heatable indoor greenhouse.
● Pricking out tool.
● Sharp garden scissors.
● Grafting knife with a bark loosening device.
● Bandage (raffia).
● Wax for cut surfaces in grafting.
● Plant labels.
● Waterproof marker for writing.

My tip: Do not try to save money when buying the knife and the scissors. Make sure you choose a good quality blade. Use a good whetstone for regular sharpening (available from most good gardening suppliers).

Trays or boxes for young plants

Special trays and boxes, made of plastic or wood, are best for starting off young seedlings or cuttings. These can be obtained in the gardening trade in different sizes. Create a sheltered mini-climate by covering the container with plastic, a pane of glass or a specially adapted hood. Indoor greenhouses consisting of a tray and a clear plastic lid to cover it are ideal. Additional floor heating that will guarantee humid and warm temperatures between 20-25°C (69-76°F) will be optimal. Also, clay or plastic pots (at least 8-10 cm/3-4 in) tall will be suitable with clay having the advantage of conducting water and allowing the pots to be watered from below.

Important: Strict hygiene should be observed for successful propagation as citrus seedlings and cuttings are extremely sensitive towards fungal infections (see pp. 56-58). Used pots should be thoroughly cleaned with hot water beforehand or dipped in a disinfectant solution (4 per cent chlorine bleach, available from chemists) for a few minutes.

My tip: Peat pellets are particularly practical for raising seedlings and cuttings. They can be bought ready to use with an accompanying mini-greenhouse in the gardening trade. After soaking them in water to make them swell up, the seeds and cuttings can be poked straight into them.

Compost for young plants

The compost used for young plants should be quite poor in nutrients and porous. Pure (river) sand is therefore best suited for raising seedlings or propagating from cuttings. The grains should be about 0.2-06 mm. Otherwise I recommend the nutrient-poor special composts available in the gardening trade (check the salt content, the EC value should be no higher than 0.5). The best material for the drainage layer is lava granules or Hortag.

Hormone rooting powder

Cuttings can be treated with hormones to encourage rooting. The bottom of the cutting should be dipped in water and then in the hormone preparation (about 1-2 cm (less than ½ - ¾ in) of the stem should be covered). The effective substance is Indolyl-butanic acid and is available in the trade.

Important: The powdered cuttings should be poked immediately into a prepared hole in the compost as the powder would otherwise be stripped off.

Spraying instead of watering

A spraying gadget is definitely recommended for careful, even moistening of the compost. You will be able to get small spray devices for the home with a capacity of 0.75-1.5 litres (1¼ - 2½ pints) or slightly larger ones that will take 5 litres (3¾ pints). The latter have the advantage of making it possible to obtain an absolutely regular distribution of drops with the help of a pump pressure device. These spray devices are also extremely good for moistening the foliage in conditions with very dry air, using water that has very little lime in it, as well as for applying plant fortifying and protection agents (see also Warning and notes, p. 61).

For the sake of order

Remember: Use plant labels and waterproof markers so that you will be able to identify the plants later on.

My tip: The classic English metal labels are particularly useful for marking large plants. They are very decorative and writing on them with a pencil couldn't be simpler. They can be used over and over again.

Propagating and grafting

Mandarins, bitter oranges and oranges are suitable for growing from seed although it may take about five to six years or longer for the first flowers to appear. Calamondin oranges, lemons and citrons are all suitable for propagating from cuttings.

Propagating from seed
Illustration 1

Always use fresh seeds from ripe fruits (store them in a cool place for a maximum of 4-5 months). Citrus fruits are cold-germinating plants, so the seed should be placed in the vegetable section of your refrigerator for a few days before planting it. An indoor greenhouse is optimal for planting (see illustration 1). First, fill the seed tray with a 2 cm (¾ in) thick drainage layer consisting of Hortag and sprinkle sand or seeding compost on top of this. Then moisten the compost thoroughly with a spray. Press the pips lightly into the compost, spacing them about 2-3 cm (¾ -1¼ in) apart and cover them with a 1-1.5 cm (less than ½ in) thick layer of propagating compost. Moisten everything again, close the cover or lid and stand the tray in a warm position. Germination will take about 30-45 days. The indoor greenhouse should, to begin with, only be opened for regular moistening with a spray device. Once the little plantlets are about 10 cm (4 in) tall, ventilate the cover for a few hours at a time to harden off the plants. Once the plants have attained a height of 30 cm (12 in), remove the cover entirely. Prick out the plants a few days later.

Pricking out
Illustration 2

For pricking out, you will need an 8-10 cm (3-4 in) wide plastic pot with a 2-3 cm (1¼ in) thick drainage layer of Hortag granules in the bottom. Then fill up the pot halfway with propagating compost. Carefully loosen the compost all around the individual plantlet in the seeding tray without damaging the very fine roots. Then, lift out the little plant and gently insert it into a previously prepared planting hole (small dibber) without bending or breaking the roots (illustration 2).
Add more propagating compost right up to the edge of the pot, then press it down firmly around the edge of the pot but more gently around the plant itself. Leave enough space for watering at the top of the pot.
Important: The neck of the root should be exactly level with the surface of the compost.

Propagating from cuttings

Propagating from citrus

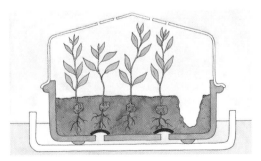

1 Planting out in an indoor greenhouse: germination takes 30-45 days. When the plants are about 30 cm (12 in) tall, remove the cover.

2 Pricking out: Carefully insert the plantlet in the prepared planting hole.

plant cuttings is not that easy. The best way is to use shoot tips that have been cut off the parts of the plant that are not yet properly woody.
A shoot tip cutting is the tip of a shoot that has no flowers or fruit. It should be cut off below the fourth or sixth leaf from the shoot tip (not counting the leaves of the shoot tip itself). The lower leaves should be removed so that three to four leaves remain on an 8-10 cm (3-4 in) long cutting. Dip the cut surface 1-2 cm (less than 1 in) deep into a rooting hormone compound. Press down lightly and moisten well (see p. 46). The temperature should be set at 25°C (76°F) and direct sunlight should be avoided. The cuttings should have formed roots after about 6-8 weeks, as soon as the leaves have begun to appear. After that, the cutting will be ready for pricking out.

Grafting
Illustration 3

Grafting is the safest and surest method of successful propagating for the hobby gardener. For this you will need a rootstock as well as a scion (a cutting with leaf buds). Japanese bitter orange (*Poncirus trifoliata*), for example, is recommended as a stock, whether you have grown this from seed yourself or whether you have obtained it from a tree nursery. It should be cut back to around 30 cm (12 in) high prior to budding. When growth restarts in the spring choose a shoot from the plant to be propagated and cut off a 10-15 cm (4-6 in) length of scionwood which contains several buds. Try to choose a young, vigorous shoot that is straight and doesn't have any branches as these are easier to work with. The diameter of the shoot should be slightly smaller than the diameter of the rootstock but as long as it isn't vastly larger the size isn't vital. Remove the leaves of the cutting and, using the grafting knife, make a horizontal slit above a leaf bud. Now remove the bud by making another cut below the leaf bud towards the first cut (see illustration

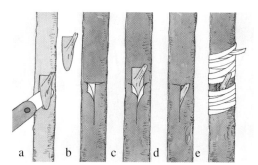

3 Make a slit above a leaf (a), carefully fold down both halves (b), insert the prepared bud in the pocket (c and d) and bandage the grafting point with raffia.

3a). The rootstock should then have a T-shaped cut made on it about 10 cm (4 in) above the soil line. The vertical cut need only be long enough to accomodate the leaf bud you have just removed, so something around 2.5 cm (1 in) should be fine. Now gently fold back the bark of the rootstock to form two flaps (illustration 3b) and then insert the prepared bud of the scion into this "pocket" and push it down far enough for the upper, straight edge to lie exactly horizontally on the T-cut (illustration 3c and 3d). For bandaging, wrap raffia around the cut, starting at the bottom but without covering the inserted bud; then bandage the upper part

(illustration 3e). The grafted plant should be stood up in a semi-shady position outside and watered normally. Also ensure there is sufficient humidity. During the growing season, remove the shoots on the stock and shorten the rapidly growing shoot to a length of 20 cm (8 in). This will result in several shoots that are then also shortened again to 20 cm (8 in) above the point where they branch. At the end of the summer, the top part of the stump of the stock should be cut off cleanly and carefully treated with tree wax.

A light winter garden room will give citrus plants the bright conditions they need.

When to overwinter

It is essential to get the climatic conditions exactly right for overwintering. While citrus plants love warmth during the growing season, they require cooler temperatures during the overwintering season.
The normal overwintering period is between the second month of autumn and the second month of spring, the time when citrus plants are in hibernation. Growth ceases for the most part and the water and nutrient requirements are reduced to a minimum.

Preparation for overwintering

Check the plants thoroughly. Cut them back slightly and remove any fruits, flowers and any weakened, sick or damaged branches, shoots and leaves. Bushes that spread a great deal, should have the main shoots cut back. The proper shaping cut will not be done until the spring (see Pruning, pp. 48/49). Prevent parasite infestation in the winter quarters by spraying the plant with 'light-medium' petroleum oil (Volk Oil). This coats and smothers the pests and is said to have low toxicity. Moisten all the parts of the plant (leaves and wood) until they are dripping. Allow to dry thoroughly before taking the plants inside.

The right temperature

The ideal overwintering temperature is about 5°C (40°F) up to a maximum of 12°C (54°F). Citrus plants that are overwintered at 5°C (40°F) are lemons (*C. limon*), bitter orange (*C. aurantium*), orange (*C. sinensis*), clementine (*C. reticulata*), mandarin (*C. reticulata*), grapefruit (*C. x paradisi*) as well as kumquat (*Fortunella*).
An exception are the Japanese bitter orange (*Poncirus trifoliata*) and the hybrids related to it. When planted out, this species will even cope with temperatures down to −30°C (−25°F) as proved by a 100-year-old specimen in the Jardin des Plantes in Paris.
Other citrus plants like it a little warmer: calamondin orange (*C. x Citrofortunella microcarpa*), lime (*C. aurantiifolia*), sweet lime (*C. limetta*), citron (*C. medica*) and pampelmousse (*C. maxima*) all like to be overwintered at temperatures between 12-16°C (54-61°F).

Light conditions

Evergreen citrus plants will need sufficient light even in winter. This is ensured in a greenhouse, a winter garden or in a position in front of a window. If only a room in a cellar is available as overwintering quarters, an artificial light source will have to supply the necessary light for twelve hours a day. Ask in the gardening trade for specially adapted fluorescent tubes which you can fix to the ceiling about 20-40 cm (8-16 in) above the plants. Switching on and off is best regulated via a time clock.

Measures of care

During the rest phase, water carefully about once or twice a month so the rootstock cannot dry out completely. Only species that like the warmth and that overwinter inside at 12-16 °C (54-61°F) should be fertilized once a month (see p. 46). You will need to ventilate the citrus plants' winter quarters daily in order to renew the oxygen supply. Be careful when the weather is very cold and frosty and when there is a sharp, cold wind. The average humidity should lie between 40 and 60 per cent. Employ humidifiers in heated living rooms or spray the plants at least once daily with water. Regular ventilating in cool overwintering rooms will prevent humidity levels from rising too high, so reducing the risk of grey mould (*Botrytis cinerea*) forming.

Care of citrus plants

Use ladybirds to combat infestation by aphids.

Ladybird larvae will consume hundreds of aphids daily.

Pests and diseases

However careful you are, you may occasionally find that pests have infested your citrus plants or that a disease has struck your plant. Aphids, for example, will often invade the balcony or patio from the garden, while scale insects and spider mites are often brought in with other pot plants. Fungal diseases are often carried through the air.

Pests

Aphids: The green citrus aphid (*Aphis citricola*), the black aphid (Aphis gossipii).

Symptoms: Curling up of leaves, sticky leaves. The aphids sit mainly on fresh shoots and leaves. Often the simultaneous appearance of black sooty mould that likes to colonize the sticky excretions of the aphids (honeydew).

Remedy: In cases of mild infestation, wash it off and perhaps remove the infested leaves and shoots. In the case of severe infestation, resort to biological pest control with ladybirds. These extremely useful creatures and their larvae in particular will consume hundreds of aphids daily.

My tip: Ladybirds and other useful insects can be obtained in the gardening trade. Contact the Henry Doubleday Research

Association (see p 62) or Fargrow Ltd for addresses in your postal area. In addition to the employment of useful insects, there is another simple and cheap solution without any risk to humans and plants – spraying with light-medium petroleum oil. Mixing ratio: 10 ml oil to 1 litre water, with a squirt of washing up liquid to aid with emulsification. After spraying, keep the plant away from direct sunlight until the leaves have dried off, otherwise there is a risk of the leaves getting burned as the drops of water react like tiny magnifying glasses. Should these natural means of controlling pests not work, you will have to resort to chemical plant protection agents. Only use preparations for controlling sucking insects on indoor plants.

Prevention: Aphids multiply rapidly in warm weather. The new shoots of plants should be checked for possible infestation particularly in the late spring.

Scale insects: *Coccus hesperidum* and other species

Symptoms: Scale insects are the greatest enemies of citrus plants. The insects that are equipped with a suction pad-like shield sit firmly without moving on woody or leafy plants and suck out the plant's juices. The plant begins to sicken, the leaves turn yellow and fall off. The first

sign of scale insects, that are rather hard to detect in the early stages, is the honeydew these insects secrete that causes the leaves and stalks to be sticky and shiny.

Remedy: The first measure is to collect the scale insects that sit quite tightly on the leaves. These creatures do, however, also tend to sit in leaf axils and shoot axils and you will not be able to find them all with the naked eye – every creature overlooked is the exit point for a new infestation of pests. At the same time, spray the plant with a spirit and soft soap solution or with petroleum oil. In cases of heavy infestation, you will not be able to avoid using a chemical treatment. In any case, you will need to repeat the measures of control several times in sequence. Scale insects are very resistant as their hard protective shield that forms with age fits snugly to the surface of the leaf so that it is not easy for the spray to reach the creature itself. The best suited agents for this particular problem are those the plant absorbs and that reach the insect through the juice it consumes from the plant itself.

Prevention: Check the undersides of leaves and stalks daily if possible for sticky secretions. Infested plants should be kept at a safe distance from the healthy ones to avoid spreading the disease from one plant to another.

Spider mites: *Panonychus ulmi* and similar species

Symptoms: spider mites are tiny insects (0.13 mm) that multiply very rapidly and will lay up to 20-50 eggs in two days when conditions suit them. The creatures prefer colonizing the axils of leaf veins, prick the veins that conduct juices and suck the juice out. Infested leaves look whitish-silvery spotted, and soon turn brown and dry up. With heavy infestation of the undersides of the leaves and above young shoots, you will be able to detect with the naked eye the finest webs in which the mites live and lay their eggs.

Remedy: You will have to react very quickly with infestation by spider mites, as the numbers of these creatures soon increase. In the early stages, it is best to cut off the infested parts of the plants. In cases of severe infestation, you can employ the natural enemy of spider mites as a biological control agent, namely, the red spider mite predator (Phytoseiulus persimilis) that will attack not only adults and kill them but also suck out the eggs.

A single red spider mite predator can suck out up to 20 eggs daily. In cases of severe infestation, only chemical plant protection agents will help.

Prevention: Dry, warm air encourages the development of spider mites, so you should

Care of citrus plants

spray your plants frequently. Weak plants and those that suffer from nutrient deficiency are infested more frequently so they need to be regularly and sufficiently fertilized.

Snails and caterpillars

Symptoms: Snails, slugs and caterpillars particularly like to attack the young leaves and shoots of citrus plants and can eat entire stalks bare overnight. Traces of feeding on young leaves and missing young shoots indicate the presence of slugs, snails or caterpillars.
Remedy: Collect the offenders; search the plant and the surrounding area, use slug pellets if necessary.
Prevention: Stand the plant containers in a position where snails cannot invade from the garden and climb up the plant (sand or water barrier). Search for caterpillars frequently.

Fungal diseases

Grey mould (Botrytis cinerea)

Symptoms: Greyish brown spots on leaves, flowers and fruit that soon spread to form a dense, grey cover of mould.
Remedy: Immediately cut off infested parts of plants and burn them so the fungus cannot spread.

Prevention: The spores of the fungus are only able to develop on dying plant tissue so sickly or diseased parts of plants should be removed at once.

Sooty mould

Symptoms: Black discolorations on leaves and stalks that occur particularly in places where the honeydew secretions of sucking insects can be found.
Remedy: Wash down the infested parts of the plants. Destroy aphids and scale insects.

Bacterial and viral diseases

These diseases are less important for the lover of ornamental citrus plants as, in the European cultivation of citrus plants, efforts are being made to cultivate only healthy, certified plant material. In order to prevent infection by sick citrus plants, imports of plants from third countries have been severely restricted since 1992.

Mistakes in care

Root rot

Symptoms: the leaves turn yellow and fade, the roots rot.
Remedy: Dry off the rootstock well, cut off decayed roots,

remove faded leaves. Repot the plant in new compost in cases of severe damage.
Prevention: Avoid waterlogging. Water little and often. Immediately pour away any excess water that collects in secondary pots or dishes underneath the main pots.

Burns

Symptoms: Yellow and brown spots on the leaves.
Remedy: Remove damaged leaves. Move the plant out of intense sunlight.
Prevention: Do not water or spray the plant in direct sunlight, allow the plant to get used to sunlight gradually after the winter rest period. Make sure that no water remains on the leaves in direct sunlight.

Nutrient deficiency

Symptoms: The leaves become pale and no new shoots appear.
Remedy: Fertilize with relevant liquid fertilizer, check the conditions in the position the plant is standing.
Prevention: Fertilize regularly, once a week during the growing season.

This combination of citrus and heliotrope smells just as beautiful as it looks.

Index

Warning and notes

This volume deals with the care of citrus plants on balconies and patios. Some of the species described here bear sharp thorns that often sit in leaf axils where they are barely visible. In the plant profiles section, this feature is specially pointed out for some species. Make particularly sure that children do not get too close to these plants. Wear gloves when handling these plants to prevent injury.

When using plant protection agents, keep to the instructions on the packaging. Store plant protection agents and fertilizers (even organic ones) in a place that is inaccessible to children and domestic pets.

Further reading

Photographic acknowledgements

The photographs in this volume are by Friedrich Strauss with the exception of:
Cover photography by L. Rose, Strauß.
Borstell: p. 2 (Kögel), 30 (Stork), 32/33 (Stork), 45 (Stork), 64/inside back cover (Stork); Photopress Bildagentur GmbH: inside front cover/p. 1 (Seve); Reinhard: p. 3 left, 5, 39 (large picture); Sammer: p. 37 right, 39 (small picture), 42 (small picture); Seethaler: p. 7; SRA-I.N.R.A./CIRAD: p. 19, 36 left, 37 left, 40 (small picture left), 41 right, 43 (small picture), 56 (top and bottom); Tintori: p. 9

Cover photographs

Front cover: *Mandarin, grapefruit - marsh, oranges - navel, Tangelo minnedla.*
Inside front cover: *Oranges on a tree.*
Back cover: *Citrus.*

This edition published 1998 by Merehurst Limited
Ferry House, 51–57 Lacy Road, Putney, London, SW15 1PR

ISBN 1 85391 669 2

A catalogue record for this book is available from the British Library.

English text copyright © Merehurst Limited 1998
Translated by Astrid Mick
Edited by Karen Douthwaite
Horticultural advisor Clive Simms
Typeset by Anita Ruddell
Printed in Hong Kong by Wing King Tong

A fascinating scent experience

he intense scent of a citrus lant can be enjoyed even on a alcony or patio, although aturally it cannot compare with he intoxicating perfumes of a un-drenched citrus plantation way from the Mediterranean eaches. The poet Alphonse Daudet wrote about the magic nd beauty of citrus plants and elieved that the only true way to xperience them was by going to he Mediterranean.